Verses of Peace

Debasish Mridha, M.D.

Illustrated by Jerry Langmaid

Epitome Publishing
4705 Towne Centre Rd. #201
Saginaw MI 48604

email sales@drmridha.com

This book is also available on Amazon.com

ISBN 978-0-9982426-1-3

Verses of Peace

What is peace? How do we attain inner peace? How do we achieve world peace? These are questions I ask myself everyday as I study the world around me. The answers to these questions require much self-awareness and soul searching.

In this book, you will find my most profound thoughts about peace. The artwork and quotes are meant to inspire you to ponder your own thoughts and beliefs about peace. It is my dearest hope that these quotes will help you to bring more peace to your heart and to the world.

Bringing peace to yourself and to those around you will help to spread peace throughout this world. The world changes every moment, and every moment can lead to a more peaceful world.

Dear Reader,

*A*s a student of the great philosophers and nature, I am always searching for the deepest truths of life. Writing has become my way of exploring the deepest thoughts and hopes of the human mind.

In my lifetime, I have been poor, and I have been wealthy. I have lived in many countries and many cultures. I have noticed that all people ask the same questions: What is peace? How do I live a peaceful life? My mission is to explore these questions in this book. My hope is that *Verses of Peace* will help you to create peace in your life and in the world.

The journey to peace begins within you. It begins with your evaluation of the definition of peace. It then moves into your thoughts about inner peace. The journey continues as you think about peace in the world. This is a never-ending journey that will help you to focus on the things that matter the most in life.

It is my utmost desire that this book will guide you and sustain you in your journey toward a lifetime of peace.

– Debasish Mridha, M.D.

Every morning the sun rises to wake you up
with a *beautiful message of peace.*

Be the *light of peace* to drive away the darkness of hatred.

You are at peace when you have *calmness in your heart,*
despite the chaos, misery, and hardships of this world.

Until we learn to love each other, understand each other, and be compassionate with each other, *peace will be an illusion*.

Peace is *truth, trust,* and *harmony*.
Peace is *joy, love,* and *great care*.

Peace begins with *nonjudgmental love*.

When we learn to be nonjudgmental with ourselves and with others in this world, *we will enjoy peace forever*.

Peace does not mean an absence of violence or conflict.

Peace is about responding to violence and conflict with love and understanding.

Hate can never eradicate hate; only *understanding* with *forgiveness* can do that.

You find peace not by looking, but *by giving*.

Every human being *desires* peace and happiness,
but only a few *strive* to attain them.

Peace is *a journey, a habit, a purpose*;
it is not merely a destination we want to reach.

Peace is not only the *goal*; it is the *game itself*.

If life is a *joyful, serious journey*, then peace
should be the train, and happiness should be the destination.

It is not very difficult to build world peace. We just have to *be kind* to each other and treat each other *with compassion*.

If you have a drop of violence or anger in
your mind, it can ignite a wildfire of violence.

Be kind.

A *simple thought* of peace or *act* of unconditional love can create mighty streams of peace.

Peace is not a condition, but it is a *perception*.
In the midst of chaos, you can be at peace in your heart.

Peace is a *process of self-realization*;
a realization that peace resides inside of us in
our inner calmness and tranquility.

Peace is a dreamland. Peace is in *my imagination*.

Peace is in *my heart*.

Peace is in *my mind*, forming a singing band.

Peace is *my best friend*, always holding my hand.

Peace is the only purpose I am fighting for with the power of *my love*.

Peace means the journey to *finding inner calmness, tranquility, and joy* in the midst of conflicts and injustices.

Practice *silence*.

Practice *patience*.

Practice *loving* everything in existence.

Peace will be there.

Peace cannot be seen with the eyes. Only the
mind can see it, and the *heart can feel it.*
Open the window of your mind to let peace come in.

When we learn to use the *power of kindness and love,*
we will fill the world with peace and happiness.

There is nothing better than love,
kindness, and forgiveness to create enduring peace.

Peace is not an option. It is the *only choice* to live a beautiful life.

To find your peace, *help others* to live in peace.

If you cannot find your inner calmness
and peace, then no one can do it for you.

When you are at peace,
the world becomes a peaceful place.

When we learn to *live in harmony with nature,*
we will learn to live in peace with each other.

Verses of Peace

Peace is present in
every breath we take.

Peace is present in every
loving gesture we make.

Peace and happiness
are more precious than land or gold.

It is easy to conform, but it takes great
courage to *stand up for peace.*

Peace is an *inner perception*
and an *inner consciousness.*

Peace is a blooming flower,
and peace is her calmness.

O my brothers and sisters of the world!

Plant the seeds of love and peace in every mind so that we may create a heavenly garden on this earth.

To promote peace,
promote understanding.

To promote understanding,
promote love.

More often than not, you are at war with yourself.
No one can really *give you peace*.

To *find peace*, you must create inner
calmness and tranquility, and practice self-love.

Life is a journey, so go on your way.
Be a *messenger of peace.*

MOUNT DISTURBANCE

PEACE MOUNTAIN

TUMULT HILL

INSECURITY RIDGE

Peace is a long journey within;
with enduring calmness, tranquility, and
kindness you will win.

The secret to happiness, peace, and self-confidence is to forgive yourself and forgive others.

Forgive yourself. Be calm and kind so that nothing will disturb your inner peace of mind.

If your mind is not at peace, *you* *cannot find it* anywhere else in the world.

To be at peace, *look inside* yourself.

Forgive your past to make peace with your present.

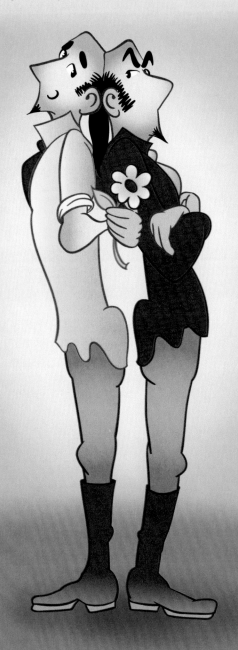

The *ultimate purpose* of life is peace and happiness.
You attain it through *service, care,* and *kindness.*

When you realize *who* you are and *why*
you're here, then you will be *at peace.*

Live your life; keep hope alive
Tomorrow will be better when peace is there.

I dream of a land of peace where everyone can *live in harmony.*

Be the source of peace and love; commit to be a person of love and kindness who *radiates peace* from within.

If you become the *light of peace*,
there will be no darkness of hatred.

Let me go where *love is abundant,*
peace is plentiful, and *joy is in the air.*

To forgive is to be free from past resentments and to *welcome the dawn of peace.*

No one is responsible for your inner peace
and inner joy, *except for you.*

Do not allow outer chaos to disturb your *inner tranquility, serenity,* and *peace.*

If you are not able to *find peace* within yourself, no one will be able to bring you peace.

Nobody can steal your *inner beauty,* *tranquility,* and *peace* without your consent.

A *simple journey* creates a peaceful life.

To bring peace to this world, you have to
be *peaceful within yourself.*

Your strength is not found in your ability to fight. It is found in your *peacefulness of mind.*

When you love those who do not deserve your love,
you create a *wave in the ocean of peace.*

When someone hurts you or hates you, do not hate them in return.
Win them with love. By doing this, *you will find peace.*

Peaceful are they who are living in the moment.

Living in the past destroys the peace of today.

Living in the future overshadows the peace of this moment.

Make peace with your past, and you will *make room* for your future.

Cleverness is egocentric and dramatic, and it gives the illusion of success.

We are always running behind it and *ultimately suffer* because of it.

However, *simplicity* is spiritual, blissful, free from drama, and joyful.

Simplicity nurtures the ultimate inner peace.

Be kind to others—not because they deserve kindness—but because you deserve inner peace.

A great way to find peace for ourselves is to *create peace* for others.

If we want peace in the world, we should *learn to love* each other.

We should know that we are *brothers* and *sisters* of the universe.

We should *teach our children* not to see differences or feel hate, but we must teach them to find harmony, coherence, and love.

A recipe for a peaceful life is to have good friends, to have positive thoughts, and to have much love in life.

To grow the flowers of peace and beauty that will make this world peaceful, you must *cultivate unconditional love* in your inner garden.

True peace can only be achieved by creating inner peace through *understanding, love,* and *forgiveness.*

Violence can never create peace.

To find your peace, *help others* to live in peace.

If you cannot find inner calmness and peace, then no one can do it for you.

When you are at peace, then the world becomes a peaceful place.

Wherever you are, whatever you are doing,
do something for peace.

Learning to forgive is the best way to find inner peace.

It is impossible to find peace in the world if we cannot
create peace within ourselves.

Inner peace does not depend on success or failure – winning or losing.

True education should teach us how to think, how to see the beauty in the midst of ugliness, how to *love without judging,* how to find opportunities to help, and how to develop a peaceful and nonviolent society.

It is *foolish to think* that we are peaceful when every day we spend more money to build killing machines than to educate our children.

For peace, let us teach *humanity,*
tolerance, and *nonviolence.*

I have a dream that one day this world will be peaceful, and people will *fight with love* not weapons.

We always *glorify war,* but why?

We have war memorials everywhere, but too few peace memorials.

We teach our children war games.

We let them play war games, but we expect peace from them.

How foolish is that?

Be an *instrument of peace,* not a preacher of hate.

Going to war to establish peace will not
bring peace. It will *just kill you.*

Human beings are *born for peace;* they like to grow up in peace.

They like to *raise their children* in peace,
and they like to *say goodbye*
to this beautiful life in peace.

Why are we always
preparing for war?

We should all have a *common goal:* to establish infinite peace in this world we call home.

We are *all connected;* our thoughts affect the whole universe.

Every *small thought of peace* will make the world a little more peaceful.

The best morning prayer
for endless peace would be:

Today *I will forgive*
everyone for their mistakes.

Today *I will love*
everyone without judging them.

Today *I will be kind* to
everyone, even if they do not deserve it.

Today *I will be a fountain*
of peace to create waves of joy
around me.

If you try to extinguish the fire of hate with the fire of anger, hate will burn the whole world.

You can only extinguish it with the water of *love*, *kindness*, and *forgiveness*.

When the waves of love extinguish the fire of resentment, the *dawn of peace on earth* will begin.

Every heart has *a song* of peace to sing;
every mind has *a story* of torment to write.

Life is transient, so leave footprints of love, kindness, and peace on the seashore of life.

Bring nothing but love and peace.
Leave nothing but beautiful memories.

I am the symbol of peace.

I am humanity.

I am the symbol of goodness.

I am community.

I am the symbol of change.

I am the light in the darkness.

I am the symbol of compassion.

I am the soul of kindness.

I am the symbol of a joyful future.

I am the symbol of unity and harmony.

I will bring brightness.

I will bring happiness.

Displays of weapons will not bring peace. Only *displays* of love and *understanding* can do that.

The war for peace can *destroy* the whole world and create a silent *emptiness*.

Play the game of peace—not the game of war.
Play, not with a gun, but with laughter.

Pay attention to peace;
peace is all that matters.

There is
and always
will be violence.

There is and always
will be agony and suffering.

In the midst of all of this we
must create and find inner peace
and spread it like a wildfire to
create a peaceful world.

Fighting for peace
is like cutting down all of
the trees to create a garden.

Even in the midst of chaos and war,
it is possible to live in peace.

Let us do more of
what brings peace to the world.

This world will find peace when *humanity wins* the world with love.

Either *give peace a chance* or suffer from the agony of war.

If peace is our ultimate goal,

love should be our only weapon.

We can bring peace into the world—not by eliminating violence in the world, but by *finding the causes of violence* and preventing them from infecting society.

Get addicted to peace!

Talk about it all day and maybe all night.

Drink it, live it, and love it. It will change the world!

Peace has no book value,
but nothing has value without peace.

When you have a choice, *choose peace.*
Nothing else really matters.

Peace is the best dress to wear.

Kindness is the best makeup for the heart.

Love is the best power to share.

Love others, not because they deserve your love, but because you want to *create enduring peace.*

The world will *see peace* when we understand that there are no enemies—just friends who don't quite understand us yet.

Violence can never wipe out violence.
Only a *caring heart* filled with love can do that.

When the *power of love* overtakes all
other power, we will find true peace on earth.

Peace is not merely the absence of war; it is the *presence of love, kindness, respect, and harmony.*

May you live in peace today and forever.

Acknowledgments

I wish to personally thank my beautiful wife and wonderful daughter for teaching me about true happiness, and for their love and support, which brings me happiness and joy every day.

I wholeheartedly appreciate Sue Wolfe and Amanda Wanless for their tireless editing and proofreading of this book. Their hard work has helped to enhance the overall purpose and content of this book.

I would also like to thank Jerry Langmaid for the beautiful artwork that reveals the essence of *Verses of Peace.*

I also want to thank my staff, Lisa MacArthur, Heather Kehoe, Melissa Baase, and Melissa Bukoski, for keeping me organized and on track.

About the Author

Dr. Debasish Mridha

Dr. Debasish Mridha is an American physician, philosopher, Poet Seer, and author. He is a seeker of the deepest truth that affects human destiny. His empowering, insightful, thought-provoking, and life-changing words have been changing human conscience every day.

"With my simple writings, I want to change the mindset of humanity so that we can create a positive new world where we can all live with dignity and peace."

– Debasish Mridha, M.D.